MY NAME IS

EVERETT ARTHUR M^cGOVERN

AND I WAS GIVEN THIS BOOK FOR
THE DAY OF MY BAPTISM ON

SUNDAY NOVEMBER 27, 2016

BY

GREAT GRANDPA & GREAT GRANDMA SWITNER

WHO WANTS ME ALWAYS TO
REMEMBER

HOW MUCH WE LOVE YOU.

Written and compiled by Sophie Piper
Illustrations copyright © 2011, 2012
Sophy Williams
This edition copyright © 2016 Lion
Hudson

The right of Sophy Williams to be
identified as the illustrator of this work has
been asserted by her in accordance with
the Copyright, Designs and Patents Act
1988.

Published by Lion Children's Books
an imprint of
Lion Hudson plc
Wilkinson House, Jordan Hill Road,
Oxford OX2 8DR, England
www.lionhudson.com/lionchildrens

ISBN 978 0 7459 7615 0

First edition 2016

Author Information
p. 12: Sarah Betts Rhodes (1829–1904)
p. 14t: Old Sarum primer (1527)
p. 22b: Julian of Norwich (1342–c.1416)
p. 34b: Victoria Tebbs
p. 39: Anonymous
p. 42t: Traditional
p. 58: St Francis of Assisi (1181–1226)
p. 60: Traditional Gaelic blessing

Acknowledgments
All unattributed prayers are by Sophie
Piper and Lois Rock, copyright © Lion
Hudson. The prayer by Victoria Tebbs is
copyright © Lion Hudson.

Bible extracts are taken or adapted from
the Good News Bible © 1994 published
by the Bible Societies/HarperCollins
Publishers Ltd UK, Good News Bible ©
American Bible Society 1966, 1971, 1976,
1992. Used with permission.

The Lord's Prayer (p. 29) as it appears
in *Common Worship: Services and Prayers
for the Church of England* (Church House
Publishing, 2000) is copyright © The
English Language Liturgical Consultation
and is reproduced by permission of the
publisher.

A catalogue record for this book is
available from the British Library

Printed and bound in China, October
2015, LH06

Prayers *and* Verses *for a* Child's Baptism

Written and compiled by Sophie Piper
Illustrated by Sophy Williams

LION
CHILDREN'S

Contents

Here I Am

Here I am
in the great big world
with everywhere to explore;
and God made me
to live as his child
and love him for evermore.

God welcomes me

One day, some people brought children to Jesus for him to place his hands on them in blessing, but the disciples scolded them.

When Jesus noticed this, he went and spoke very firmly to his disciples.

"What you did was not right," he told them. "Let the children come to me, and do not stop them, because the kingdom of God belongs to such as these.

"You can be sure of this: whoever does not accept the invitation to the kingdom of God like a child will never enter it."

Then he took the children in his arms, placed his hands on each of them, and blessed them.

FROM MARK CHAPTER 10, VERSES 13 TO 17

God cares for me

God, who made the earth,
The air, the sky, the sea,
Who gave the light its birth,
Careth for me.

God, who made the grass,
The flower, the fruit, the tree,
The day and night to pass,
Careth for me.

God, who made all things,
On earth, in air, in sea,
Who changing seasons brings,
Careth for me.

Jesus said...

"For only a penny you can buy two sparrows, yet not one sparrow falls to the ground without your Father God allowing it.

"So do not be afraid; you are worth much more than many sparrows!"

FROM MATTHEW CHAPTER 10, VERSES 29 AND 31

God guides me

God be in my head, and in my understanding;
God be in my eyes, and in my looking;
God be in my mouth, and in my speaking;
God be in my heart, and in my thinking;
God be at my end, and at my departing.

God will always be near to you, and you will not have to search for him.

If you wander off the road to the right or the left, you will hear his voice behind you saying, "Here is the road, follow it."

FROM ISAIAH CHAPTER 30, VERSES 20 AND 21

I will choose the narrow path,
I will walk the straight,
Through the wide and winding world
Up to heaven's gate.

Thinking About God

Dear God, you are my shepherd,
You give me all I need,
You take me where the grass grows green
And I can safely feed.

You take me where the water
Is quiet and cool and clear;
And there I rest and know I'm safe
For you are always near.

BASED ON PSALM 23

Praising God

Praise the Lord from heaven,
all beings of the height!
Praise him, holy angels
and golden sun so bright.

Praise him, silver moonlight,
praise him, every star!
Let your praises shine
throughout the universe so far.

Praise the Lord from earth below,
all beings of the deep!
Lightning, flash! You thunder, roar!
You ocean creatures, leap.

Praise him, hill and mountain!
Praise him, seed and tree.
Praise him, all you creatures
that run the wide world free.

Let the mighty praise him.
Let the children sing.
Men and women, young and old:
Praise your God and king.

FROM PSALM 148

Pleasing God

The Lord has his throne in heaven.
He watches people everywhere
and knows what they are doing.

He sees the wicked, and his heart is against them.

He sees the righteous and loves their good deeds.

FROM PSALM 11

Who may come into God's presence?

The person who obeys God in everything,
who always speaks the truth,
who keeps every promise,
who cannot be lured into doing wrong.

Such a person will be safe all through life.

FROM PSALM 15

Happy are those who find joy in obeying the
Law of the Lord.
They are like trees that grow beside a stream,
that bear fruit at the right time,
and whose leaves do not dry up.
They succeed in everything they do.

FROM PSALM 1, VERSES 1 TO 3

Trusting God

Dear God,
Help me not to be proud.
Help me not to think more highly of myself than
   is right.
Help me to trust in you
  that I may be content and at peace:
  like a child in its mother's arms.

BASED ON PSALM 131

O God,
as truly as you are our father,
so just as truly you are our mother.
We thank you, God our father,
for your strength and goodness.
We thank you, God our mother,
for the closeness of your caring.
O God, we thank you for the great love
you have for each one of us.

Thinking About Jesus

I'm learning to be more like Jesus,
I'm learning the right way to live.
I'm learning to show loving kindness,
I'm learning to truly forgive.

Learning from Jesus

Jesus said...

"The most important commandment is this: 'Love the Lord your God with all your heart, with all your soul, with all your mind, and with all your strength.'

   "The second most important commandment is this: 'Love your neighbour as you love yourself.'"

<small>FROM MARK CHAPTER 12, VERSES 29 TO 31</small>

Jesus said ...

"And now I give you a new commandment: love one another. As I have loved you, so you must love one another."

<small>JOHN CHAPTER 13, VERSE 34</small>

Jesus said…

"I am the light of the world. Whoever follows me will have the light of life and will never walk in darkness."

JOHN CHAPTER 8, VERSE 12

Jesus, you are the light of the world.
May we live our lives as you taught, so that your light will shine through us in all we think and say and do.

Praying with Jesus

Jesus often spent time alone praying. One day, when he had finished, a disciple said this to him:

"Lord, teach us to pray."

FROM LUKE CHAPTER 11, VERSE 1

Jesus gave them this prayer:

Our Father in heaven,
hallowed be your name,
your kingdom come,
your will be done,
on earth as in heaven.
Give us today our daily bread.
Forgive us our sins
as we forgive those who sin against us.
Lead us not into temptation
but deliver us from evil.

FROM MATTHEW CHAPTER 6, VERSES 9 TO 13
AND LUKE CHAPTER 11, VERSES 2 TO 4

Following Jesus

Lord Jesus, who died upon the cross:
You know this world's suffering,
You know this world's sorrowing,
You know this world's dying.

In your name, Lord Jesus, who rose again:
I will work for this world's healing,
I will work for this world's rejoicing,
I will work for this world's living.

In the Easter garden the leaves are turning green;
in the Easter garden the risen Lord is seen.
In the Easter garden we know that God above
brings us safe to heaven through Jesus and his love.

Thinking About the Holy Spirit

Let the Spirit come
like the winds that blow:
take away my doubts;
help my faith to grow.

Let the Spirit come
like a flame of gold:
warm my soul within;
make me strong and bold.

33

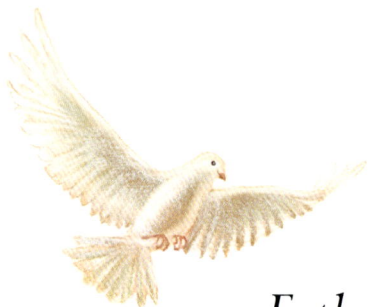

Father, Son, Spirit

Jesus said to his disciples…

"Go to all peoples everywhere and make them my disciples: baptize them in the name of the Father, the Son, and the Holy Spirit, and teach them to obey everything I have commanded you."

FROM MATTHEW CHAPTER 28, VERSES 19 TO 20

All glory to the Father,
All glory to the Son,
All glory to the Spirit:
God in three, yet one.

Changed by God's Spirit

Spirit of God, put love in my life.
Spirit of God, put joy in my life.
Spirit of God, put peace in my life.

Spirit of God, make me patient.
Spirit of God, make me kind.
Spirit of God, make me good.

Spirit of God, give me faithfulness.
Spirit of God, give me humility.
Spirit of God, give me self-control.

*Based on Galatians chapter 5,
verses 22 to 23*

Love

Help me, Lord, to show your love.

Help me to be patient and kind, not jealous
or conceited or proud. May I never be
ill-mannered, selfish or irritable; may I be quick
to forgive and forget.

May I not gloat over wrongdoing, but rather be glad about
things that are good and true.

May I never give up loving: may my faith and hope and
patience never come to an end.

BASED ON *1 CORINTHIANS CHAPTER 13, VERSES 4 TO 7*

Love is giving, not taking,
mending, not breaking,
trusting, believing,
never deceiving,
patiently bearing
and faithfully sharing
each joy, every sorrow,
today and tomorrow.

Learning to Pray

Jesus said…

"Ask, and you will receive;
seek, and you will find;
knock, and the door will be opened to you.

"For everyone who asks will receive,
and anyone who seeks will find,
and the door will be opened to those who knock.

"Your Father in heaven will give good things to
those who ask him."

FROM MATTHEW CHAPTER 7,
VERSES 7 TO 8 AND 11

Thank-you prayers

Thank you, God in heaven,
For a day begun.
Thank you for the breezes,
Thank you for the sun.
For this time of gladness,
For our work and play,
Thank you, God in heaven,
For another day.

Thank you for the little things
we notice every day
that shine on earth with heaven's gold
and cheer us on our way.

Sorry prayers

I told God everything:
I told God about all the wrong things I had done.
I gave up trying to pretend.
I gave up trying to hide.
I knew the only thing to do was to confess.

And God forgave me.

BASED ON PSALM 32, VERSE 5

Take my wrongdoing
and throw it away,
down in the deep of the sea;
welcome me into your kingdom of love
for all of eternity.

Based on Micah chapter 7, verses 18 to 20

45

Asking prayers

Help us not to worry, dear God.
Remind us to ask you for the things we need
and give thanks.

Give us the peace that comes from knowing that all
our worries are safe with you.

FROM PHILIPPIANS CHAPTER 4, VERSES 6 TO 7

God is our shelter and strength,
always ready to help in times of trouble.
So we will not be afraid, even if the earth is shaken
and mountains fall into the ocean depths;
even if the seas roar and rage,
and the hills are shaken.

PSALM 46, VERSES 1 TO 3

Living the Christian Life

Dear God,
Even though I am only a child
people can tell what I am like by what I do.

Please make me honest and good.

BASED ON PROVERBS CHAPTER 20, VERSE 11

Seeing Jesus in others

Lord Jesus,
Make me as kind to others
as I would want to be to you.

Make me as generous to others
as I would want to be to you.

May I take time to help them
as I would take time to help you.

May I take trouble to help them
as I would take trouble to help you.

May I look into the faces of those I meet
and see your face.

Based on Matthew chapter 25, verses 37 to 40

Dear God,
Help me to love my enemies.
Show me how to do good things
    for those who hurt me.
Remind me to pray for those who are unkind.

Based on Luke chapter 6, verses 27 to 28

Speaking gently

Dear God,
May I learn to say what is right and true without anger
and without spitefulness.

Dear God,
If people speak to me with angry words
may I listen quietly
and give a gentle answer
that may end the quarrel between us.

Words can make us happy
Words can make us sad
Words can leave us feeling calm
WORDS CAN MAKE US MAD!
So we must be careful
In the things we say
Dear God, help us choose the words
That we use today.

Forgiving others

Jesus said…

"If you forgive others the wrongs they have done to you, your Father in heaven will forgive you."

MATTHEW CHAPTER 6, VERSE 14

Seven
times seven
I freely forgive
and seven
times seventy more.
Lord, give me the grace
to forgive
and forgive,
again
and again
I implore.

BASED ON MATTHEW CHAPTER 18, VERSES 21 TO 35

As Night Falls

May the Lord bless you.
May the Lord take care of you.
May the light of his goodness
   always shine upon you.
May you enjoy good things.
May you live in peace.

BASED ON NUMBERS CHAPTER 6,
VERSES 24 TO 26

Peace in my heart

Send your peace into my heart, O Lord,
that I may be contented
with your mercies of this day
and confident of your protection for this night;
and having forgiven others,
even as you have forgiven me,
may I go to my rest in peaceful trust
through Jesus Christ, our Lord. Amen.

Peace through the night

Deep peace of the running waves to you,
Deep peace of the flowing air to you,
Deep peace of the quiet earth to you,
Deep peace of the shining stars to you,
Deep peace of the shades of night to you,
Moon and stars always giving light to you,
Deep peace of Christ, the Son of Peace, to you.

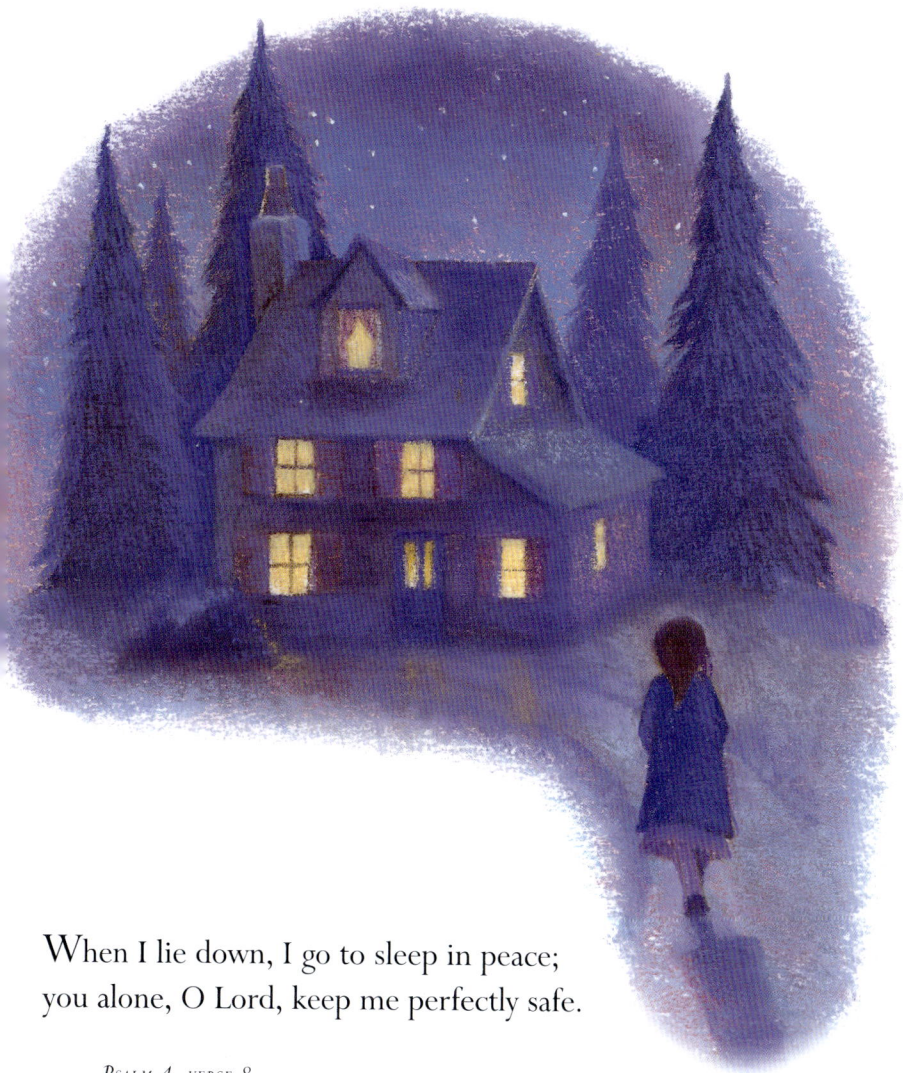

When I lie down, I go to sleep in peace;
you alone, O Lord, keep me perfectly safe.

PSALM 4, VERSE 8

61

On the day of my baptism people gathered together. They promised they would help me to grow up to know God's love and goodness.

_____

_____

_____

_____

_____

_____

_____